Teach Your Kids About Countries

[Vol2]

[ZHINGOORA BOOKS]

Armenia

Aruba

Ashmore and Cartier Islands

Australia

Austria

Azerbaijan

Bahamas

Bahrain

Bangladesh

Barbados

Armenia

Background:

Armenia prides itself on being the first nation to formally adopt Christianity (early 4th century). Despite periods of autonomy, over the centuries Armenia came under the sway of various empires including the Roman, Byzantine, Arab, Persian, and Ottoman. During World War I in the western portion of Armenia, Ottoman Turkey instituted a policy of forced resettlement coupled with other harsh practices that resulted in an estimated 1 million Armenian deaths. The eastern area of Armenia was ceded by the Ottomans to Russia in 1828; this portion declared its independence in 1918, but was conquered by the Soviet Red Army in 1920. Armenian leaders remain preoccupied by the long conflict with Azerbaijan over Nagorno-Karabakh, a primarily Armenian-populated region, assigned to Soviet Azerbaijan in the 1920s by Moscow. Armenia and Azerbaijan began fighting over the area in 1988; the struggle escalated after both countries attained independence from the Soviet Union in 1991. By May 1994, when a cease-fire took hold, ethnic Armenian forces held not only Nagorno-Karabakh but also a significant portion of Azerbaijan proper. The economies of both sides have been hurt by their inability to make substantial progress toward a peaceful resolution. Turkey closed the common border with Armenia in 1994 because of the Armenian separatists' control of Nagorno-Karabakh and surrounding areas, further hampering Armenian economic growth. In 2009, senior Armenian leaders began pursuing rapprochement with Turkey, aiming to secure an opening of the border; this process is currently dormant.

Aruba

Background:

Discovered and claimed for Spain in 1499, Aruba was acquired by the Dutch in 1636. The island's economy has been dominated by three main industries. A 19th century gold rush was followed by prosperity brought on by the opening in 1924 of an oil refinery. The last decades of the 20th century saw a boom in the tourism industry. Aruba seceded from the Netherlands Antilles in 1986 and became a separate, autonomous member of the Kingdom of the Netherlands. Movement toward full independence was halted at Aruba's request in 1990.

Ashmore and Cartier Islands

Background:

These uninhabited islands came under Australian authority in 1931; formal administration began two years later. Ashmore Reef supports a rich and diverse avian and marine habitat; in 1983, it became a National Nature Reserve. Cartier Island, a former bombing range, became a marine reserve in 2000.

Australia

Background:

Aboriginal settlers arrived on the continent from Southeast Asia about 40,000 years before the first Europeans began exploration in the 17th century. No formal territorial claims were made until 1770, when Capt. James COOK took possession in the name of Great Britain. Six colonies were created in the late 18th and 19th centuries; they federated and became the Commonwealth of Australia in 1901. The new country took advantage of its natural resources to rapidly develop agricultural and manufacturing industries and to make a major contribution to the British effort in World Wars I and II. In recent decades, Australia has transformed itself into an internationally competitive, advanced market economy. It boasted one of the OECD's fastest growing economies during the 1990s, a performance due in large part to economic reforms adopted in the 1980s. Long-term concerns include climate-change issues such as the depletion of the ozone layer and more frequent droughts, and management and conservation of coastal areas, especially the Great Barrier Reef.

Austria

Background:

Once the center of power for the large Austro-Hungarian Empire, Austria was reduced to a small republic after its defeat in World War I. Following annexation by Nazi Germany in 1938 and subsequent occupation by the victorious Allies in 1945, Austria's status remained unclear for a decade. A State Treaty signed in 1955 ended the occupation, recognized Austria's independence, and forbade unification with Germany. A constitutional law that same year declared the country's "perpetual neutrality" as a condition for Soviet military withdrawal. The Soviet Union's collapse in 1991 and Austria's entry into the European Union in 1995 have altered the meaning of this neutrality. A prosperous, democratic country, Austria entered the EU Economic and Monetary Union in 1999.

Azerbaijan

Background.

Azerbaijan - a nation with a majority-Turkic and majority-Muslim population - was briefly independent from 1918 to 1920; it regained its independence after the collapse of the Soviet Union in 1991. Despite a 1994 cease-fire, Azerbaijan has yet to resolve its conflict with Armenia over Nagorno-Karabakh, a primarily Armenian-populated region that Moscow recognized as part of Soviet Azerbaijan in the 1920s after Armenia and Azerbaijan disputed the status of the territory. Armenia and Azerbaijan began fighting over the area in 1988; the struggle escalated after both countries attained independence from the Soviet Union in 1991. By May 1994, when a cease-fire took hold, ethnic Armenian forces held not only Nagorno-Karabakh but also seven surrounding provinces in the territory of Azerbaijan. Corruption in the country is ubiquitous, and the government, which eliminated presidential term limits in a 2009 referendum, has been accused of authoritarianism. Although the poverty rate has been reduced in recent years due to revenue from oil production, the promise of widespread wealth resulting from the continued development of Azerbaijan's energy sector remains largely unfulfilled.

Bahamas

Background:

Lucayan Indians inhabited the islands when Christopher COLUMBUS first set foot in the New World on San Salvador in 1492. British settlement of the islands began in 1647; the islands became a colony in 1783. Since attaining independence from the UK in 1973, The Bahamas has prospered through tourism and international banking and investment management. Because of its geography, the country is a major transshipment point for illegal drugs, particularly shipments to the US and Europe, and its territory is used for smuggling illegal migrants into the US.

Bahrain

Background:

In 1783, the al-Khalifa family captured Bahrain from the Persians.In order to secure these holdings, it entered into a series of treaties with the UK during the 19th century that made Bahrain a British protectorate. The archipelago attained its independence in 1971. Bahrain's small size and central location among Persian Gulf countries require it to play a delicate balancing act in foreign affairs among its larger neighbors. Facing declining oil reserves, Bahrain has turned to petroleum processing and refining and has transformed itself into an international banking center. King HAMAD bin Isa al-Khalifa, after coming to power in 1999, pushed economic and political reforms to improve relations with the Shia community. Shia political societies participated in 2010 parliamentary and municipal elections. Al Wifaq, the largest Shia political society, won the largest number of seats in the elected chamber of the legislature. However, Shia discontent has resurfaced in recent years with street demonstrations and occasional low-level violence.

Bangladesh

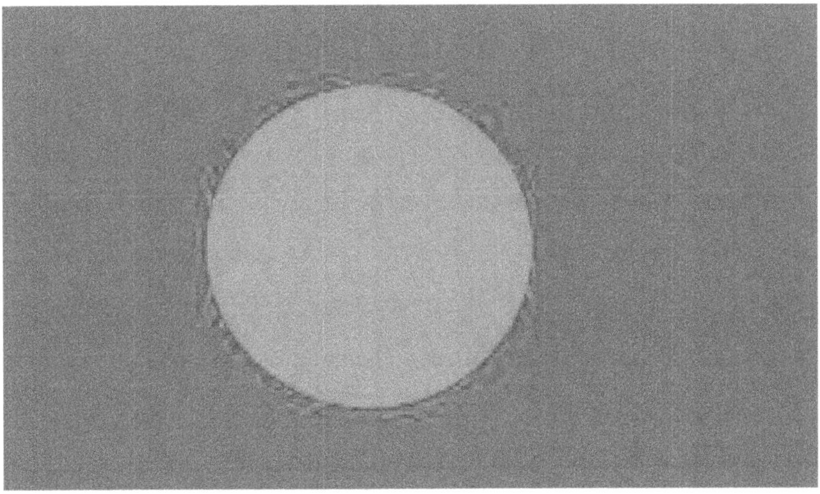

Background:

Europeans began to set up trading posts in the area of Bangladesh in the 16th century; eventually the British came to dominate the region and it became part of British India. In 1947, West Pakistan and East Bengal (both primarily Muslim) separated from India (largely Hindu) and jointly became the new country of Pakistan. East Bengal became East Pakistan in 1955, but the awkward arrangement of a two-part country with its territorial units separated by 1,600 km left the Bengalis marginalized and dissatisfied. East Pakistan seceded from its union with West Pakistan in 1971 and was renamed Bangladesh. A military-backed, emergency caretaker regime suspended parliamentary elections planned for January 2007 in an effort to reform the political system and root out corruption. In contrast to the strikes and violent street rallies that had marked Bangladeshi politics in previous years, the parliamentary elections finally held in late December 2008 were mostly peaceful and Sheikh HASINA Wajed was elected prime minister. About a third of this extremely poor country floods annually during the monsoon rainy season, hampering economic development.

Barbados

Background:

The island was uninhabited when first settled by the British in 1627. Slaves worked the sugar plantations established on the island until 1834 when slavery was abolished. The economy remained heavily dependent on sugar, rum, and molasses production through most of the 20th century. The gradual introduction of social and political reforms in the 1940s and 1950s led to complete independence from the UK in 1966. In the 1990s, tourism and manufacturing surpassed the sugar industry in economic importance.

The End

www.ingramcontent.com/pod-product-compliance
Lightning Source LLC
Chambersburg PA
CBHW060023300526
45794CB00003B/1275
9781480268166